The Ultimate Guacamole Cookbook

The Secret to Great Recipes - Avocados Of Course!

By: Owen Davis

Copyright © 2022 by Owen Davis.

Copyright Notice!

Please don't reproduce this book, guys! My team and I have worked long and hard to get the best quality content out there (this book!), and now that we have, we'd like to take care of it—but we need your help to do it. That means you aren't allowed to make any print or electronic reproductions, sell, re-publish, or distribute this book in parts or as a whole unless you have express written consent from me or my team.

While we have gone to great lengths to make sure the information presented is clear and precise, I nor any part of my team can be held liable for any damages or accidents that occur from any interpretations of this book. If you are unsure how to carry out certain steps from our recipes, look up videos or tutorials online to get a better understanding of how to do something. Remember that being in the kitchen always comes with certain risks, so take things easy and stay safe!

Table of Contents

Introduction 7

The Benefits of Guacamole Recipes 8

The Guacamole Recipes 9

   1. Sweet and Spicy Mango Avocado Guacamole 10

   2. Festive Guacamole 12

   3. Cucumber Avocado Pineapple Guacamole 14

   4. Roasted Cherry Tomato Guacamole 16

   5. Fruity Guacamole Blend 18

   6. Cucumber Guacamole 20

   7. Romano and Lime Black Bean Guacamole 22

   8. Chunky Guacamole 24

   9. Citrus Lobster Guacamole 26

   10. Tomatillo Guacamole 28

   11. Guacamole with Wasabi and Japanese Mayonnaise 30

   12. Devilled Eggs with Guacamole 32

   13. Pomegranate Guacamole 34

   14. Prawn and Dill Guacamole 36

   15. Pumpkin Guacamole 38

16. Spring Pea and Mint Guacamole 40

17. Summer Stone Fruit Guacamole 42

18. Toasted Pepita and Cotija Cheese Guacamole 44

19. Tuna Guacamole 46

20. Italian-Style Guacamole 48

21. Crab Guacamole 50

22. Fajita Guacamole 52

23. Shrimp Guacamole 54

24. Black Bean Guacamole 56

25. Strawberry Guacamole 58

26. Guacamole Hummus 60

27. Chicken & Guacamole Tostadas 62

28. Honey & Raisin Guacamole Dessert 64

29. Sweet Guacamole Dessert 66

30. Guacamole Veggie Wraps 68

31. Lemon Pepper Shrimp and Guacamole Rolls 70

32. Guacamole Deviled Eggs 72

33. Mushroom & Guacamole Tacos 74

34. Kyle's Smokey Chardonnay Guacamole 76

35. Ensalada De Guacamole 78

36. Garbonzo Guacamole Dip 80

37. Green Chili Pepper Guacamole 82

38. Guacamole Cocktail Spread 84

39. Guacamole Colombo 86

40. Guacamole Cream Soup 88

41. Broccoli Guacamole 90

42. Best-ever Guacamole 92

43. Best Guacamole Dip 94

44. Blender Guacamole 96

45. California Guacamole 98

46. Guacamole Bean Casserole Dip 100

47. Guacamole Burgers 102

48. Nicole's Amazing Guacamole 104

49. Vegetable Guacamole 106

50. Ambrosia South American Guacamole 108

51. Tomato - Salsa Guacamole 110

52. Cajun Guacamole 112

53. Choice Mango Chipotle Guacamole 114

54. Heavenly Guasacaca - Guacamole from Venezuela 116

55. Inviting Fruity Guacamole 118

56. Tantalizing Haphazard Guacamole 120

Conclusion 122

About the Author 123

Appendices 124

Introduction

Do you have an avocado tree in your yard (or do you know someone who does)? If so, congratulations: you are the proud owner of a bounty! You might not know it, but avocados require surprisingly little work to grow and maintain. If you're growing them yourself and want to reap some tasty rewards, this is the perfect book for you.

If you don't grow avocados, you might have several questions about harvesting them, storing them, and using them in recipes. This cookbook gives you the perfect guide for preparing wonderful recipes using avocados.

The Benefits of Guacamole Recipes

If you're looking for a great cookbook that teaches you how to make great guacamole, look no further than the Guacamole Cookbook. This book is full of recipes, tips, and tricks that will get you on the path to making the most delicious guacamole possible. It's also packed with delicious, tangy and fresh ingredients. We recommend it for beginners.

The guacamole in this cookbook should be chunky, but not too smooth. The right consistency is when more large pieces remain than mashed parts. You can adjust the amount of lime, peppers, and oil according to your taste. If you want more zing, add tabasco. If you prefer less spice, add a pinch of cayenne pepper.

Once made, guacamole will stay fresh in the fridge for three to four days. If it's refrigerated, it'll keep its green color for about six to eight hours. You can also keep it for a few more days. A great tip for keeping guacamole fresh is to cover it with plastic wrap. When you're making guacamole, don't forget to add lime to it.

The world is a melting pot of cultures. Different people from different places have different tastes, habits and beliefs. One of the greatest things about being part of a huge world is that we get to taste the delicacies of so many places without even having to move. That's one reason why food is such an important part of every culture. Each place has its own set of food recipes, vegetables, herbs and spices that are used in every dish prepared by the natives of that place.

Guacamole is one such recipe that has gained a lot of popularity in recent years. This Mexican dish is one of the most famous recipes prepared in Mexico. It originated in the region of Puebla, Mexico. In fact, it is so famous that it has become part of the diet of many people across the globe as well. Guacamole recipes are prepared using avocados, which are extensively cultivated in many parts of Mexico, especially Puebla. These plants are also grown in many parts of the world, such as in the United States and Canada. Avocados are one of the most delicious, nutritious and versatile fruits that is rich in essential vitamins and minerals!

The Guacamole Recipes

These are great treats that are made by combining avocados with onions, tomatoes, peppers and other spices. This is a healthy dish that can be consumed with a variety of ingredients. The main ingredient used in this recipe is avocados. This is one of the most delicious recipes and has been very popular for a long time. There are many variations of this recipe, but it all has the same basic elements.

1. Sweet and Spicy Mango Avocado Guacamole

This guacamole gets its sweetness from the ripe mangoes and some spiciness from the smoked paprika. The tomatoes are optional to add to this recipe.

Servings: 2

Preparation time: 5 minutes

Ingredients:

- ½ c. Mango cubes
- 1 c. Avocado puree
- 1 tomato, cut into matchsticks
- 1 tsp. Smoked paprika
- ¼ tsp. Salt
- ¼ tsp. Pepper
- 1 tbsp. Olive oil
- 1 tbsp. Lime juice
- 1 tsp. Chopped cilantro

Directions:

First, in a mixing bowl, add the avocado puree.

Add the olive oil, lime juice, salt, pepper, and cilantro.

Next, mix well. Add the mango cubes and tomatoes.

Sprinkle the paprika on top and serve.

2. Festive Guacamole

It is not your average guacamole recipe! Instead, it calls for a celebration to make this recipe because it contains many ingredients that make it unique and special.

Servings: 2

Preparation time: 5 minutes

Ingredients:

- 1 c. Ripe avocado cubes
- 1 tsp. Olive oil
- ½ c. Pomegranate seeds
- 2 tbsps. Crumbled cheddar cheese
- 2 tbsps. Chopped & toasted pistachios
- ¼ tsp. Salt
- ¼ tsp. Pepper
- 2 tbsps. Lime juice
- 1 tsp. Chopped coriander
- 1 tsp. Chopped cilantro

Directions:

In a mixing bowl, mash the avocado cubes.

Add the olive oil, salt, pepper, and lime juice and mix well.

Add the cilantro and coriander and mix well.

Top with the pomegranate seeds, cheese, and pistachios. Serve.

3. Cucumber Avocado Pineapple Guacamole

It is simple chunky guacamole with English cucumber, red onion, and pineapple. The taste of it is refreshing and light.

Servings: 2

Preparation time: 5 minutes

Ingredients:

- ½ c. pineapple cubes
- 1 chopped red onion
- 1 cubed avocado
- 2 chopped English cucumbers
- 1 tbsp. Chopped cilantro
- 1 tbsp. Lime juice
- ½ tsp. Salt
- ¼ tsp. Pepper
- 1 chopped jalapeno

Directions:

In a bowl, combine the avocado with the pineapple cubes and onion.

Add the cucumber, jalapeno, and cilantro, and mix well.

Add the lime juice, salt, and pepper. Mix again and serve.

4. Roasted Cherry Tomato Guacamole

It is a unique guacamole recipe with roasted cherry tomatoes, basil, lime, and avocado coming together into one bowl. It can serve as a side, snack, or main course.

Servings: 2

Preparation time: 15 minutes

Ingredients:

- 1 tbsp. Olive oil
- 1 tbsp. Chopped basil
- 2 tbsps. Lime juice
- ½ c. Sliced cherry tomatoes
- 1 c. Avocado cubes
- ½ tsp. Minced rosemary
- ¼ tsp. Salt
- ¼ tsp. Pepper

Directions:

Sprinkle the salt, pepper, and rosemary onto the cherry tomatoes.

Roast them with olive oil for 5 minutes.

In a bowl, mash the avocado cubes.

Add the lime juice, salt, and pepper, and mix well.

Add the roasted cherry tomatoes and basil, and serve.

5. Fruity Guacamole Blend

This recipe is a healthy fix as it is full of fruits. It only takes two preparation steps to get the fantastic guacamole meal ready.

Servings: 6

Preparation time: 10 minutes

Ingredients:

- 1 peeled, pitted & diced avocado
- 1½ tsps. minced red onion
- 1 tsp. seeded & finely chopped serrano chile
- 12 seedless halved red grapes
- 12 seedless halved green grapes
- ½ c. diced peaches
- 1 tsp. Salt

Directions:

Combine all ingredients in a bowl.

Mix well and chill before serving.

6. Cucumber Guacamole

In this fantastic cucumber guacamole, you blend avocado, cucumber, onion, bell pepper, mint, yogurt, olive oil, lemon juice, garlic, pepper, and salt to make a satisfying dish. Try cooking this recipe for breakfast or dinner or dessert, or snack.

Servings: 4

Preparation time: 10 minutes

Ingredients:

- 1 peeled, seeded & chopped cucumber
- 1 peeled, pitted & cubed avocado
- 1 tbsp. finely chopped onion
- 1 tbsp. finely chopped green bell pepper
- 2 tsps. finely chopped mint
- ½ c. plain Greek yogurt
- ¼ c. olive oil
- 2 tbsps. lemon juice
- 1 minced garlic clove
- ½ tsp. Salt
- ¼ tsp. Pepper

Directions:

Combine the ingredients in a food processor.

Process the mixture.

Chill before serving.

7. Romano and Lime Black Bean Guacamole

The preparation of this recipe is simple and takes only 10 minutes to get ready. You can serve it as a side dish.

Servings: 6

Preparation time: 10 minutes

Ingredients:

- 3 peeled, pitted & mashed large avocados
- ½ c. finely chopped chives
- ¼ c. finely chopped cilantro
- 2 finely chopped garlic cloves
- 1 tbsp. lime juice
- 2 c. rinsed & drained black beans
- 1½ c. grated Romano cheese
- 2 diced tomatoes
- 1 tbsp. cayenne pepper

Directions:

Combine the ingredients in a food processor.

Process the mixture.

Chill before serving.

8. Chunky Guacamole

This tasty guacamole recipe will leave you yearning for more. It is even more interesting that the instructions are easy to follow, and the results are excellent.

Servings: 6

Preparation time: 10 minutes

Ingredients:

- 2 ripe avocados
- 1 whole, red tomato, seeds out, cut into small dice
- 1 minced red onion
- 2 minced garlic cloves
- Juice of 1 lime
- 1 tsp. Salt
- 1 tsp. Black pepper

Directions:

Slice the avocados into half, then eliminate the seed and scrape the avocado meat from its skin.

Place in a mortar and smash with the pestle with the garlic. Add juice.

Add sliced onions and tomatoes and mix with a spoon only.

Season with salt and pepper. Serve.

9. Citrus Lobster Guacamole

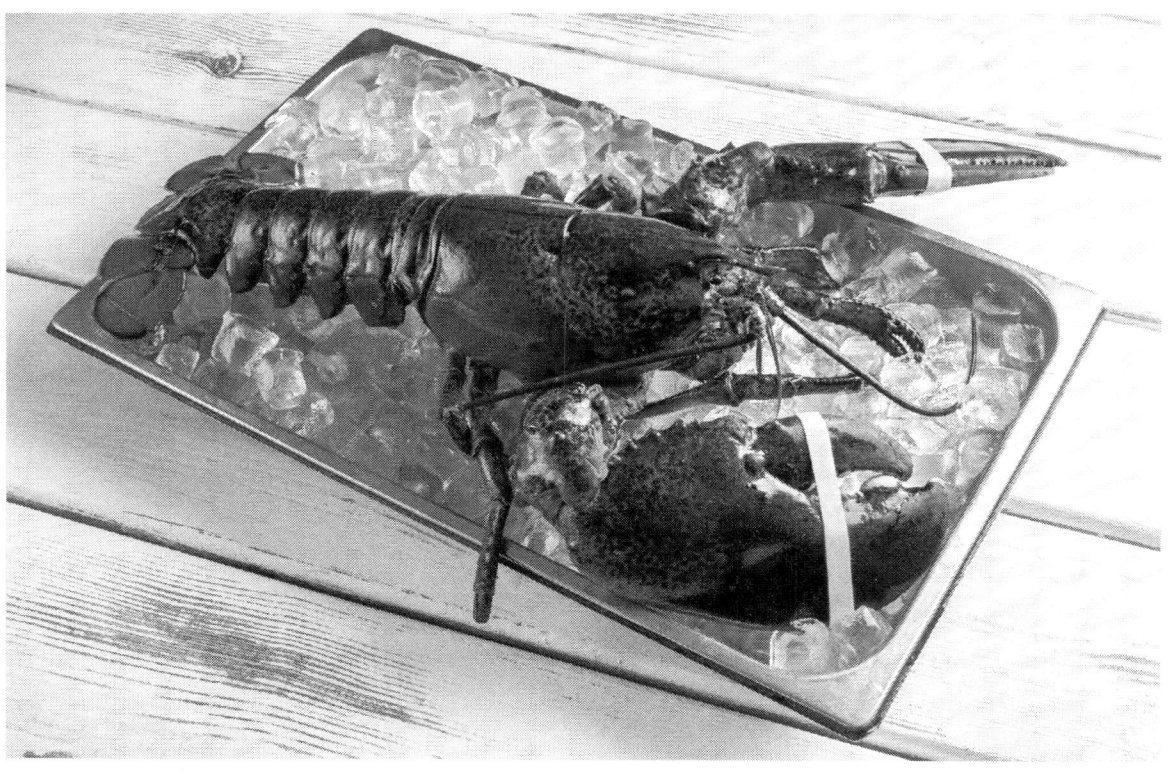

Elevate your parties by preparing this delicious cocktail fixture or appetizer. You can find the ingredients at local stores, so nothing stops you now.

Servings: 6

Preparation time: 30 minutes

Ingredients:

- 1 tbsp. olive oil
- 3 Maine lobster tails
- 1 tsp. lemon zest
- Juice of 1 lemon
- 2 ripe avocados
- 1 whole, red tomato, seeds out, cut into small dice
- 1 minced red onion
- 2 minced garlic cloves
- Juice of 1 lime
- 1 tsp. Salt
- 1 tsp. Black pepper

Directions:

Drizzle lobster tails with olive oil in a griller, and season with salt and pepper. Place on grill and cook lobster tails. Remove from shells and roughly chop leaving chunks.

Slice the avocados into half, then eliminate the seed and scrape the avocado meat from its skin.

Place this in a food processor with the remaining ingredients. Add lobster chunks.

Season with salt and pepper. Serve.

10. Tomatillo Guacamole

Another perfect combination! Tomatillo has the body to give guacamole the ideal texture and taste.

Servings: 6

Preparation time: 10 minutes

Ingredients:

- 2 ripe avocados
- 2 husked & boiled tomatillos
- 1 red tomato, seeds out, cut into small dice
- 1 minced red onion
- 2 minced garlic cloves
- Juice of 1 lime
- Salt
- 1 tsp. Black pepper

Directions:

Slice the avocados into half, then eliminate the seed and scrape the avocado meat from its skin.

Place this in a food processor with the remaining ingredients.

Season with salt and pepper. Serve.

11. Guacamole with Wasabi and Japanese Mayonnaise

This Asian take on guacamole is a sure hit. The sting of wasabi and mellow flavors of Japanese mayonnaise is perfect for making that creamy guacamole with the right amount of kick.

Servings: 6

Preparation time: 10 minutes

Ingredients:

- 2 ripe avocados
- 1 whole, red tomato, seeds out, cut into small dice
- 1 minced red onion
- 2 minced garlic cloves
- Juice of 1 lime
- 2 tsps. wasabi paste
- ¼ c. Japanese mayonnaise
- 1 tsp. Salt
- 1 tsp. Black pepper
- 1 thinly sliced Nori sheet

Directions:

Slice the avocados into half, then eliminate the seed. Next, scrape the avocado meat from its skin.

Place this in a food processor with the remaining ingredients.

Season with salt and pepper.

Sprinkle with Nori on top. Serve.

12. Devilled Eggs with Guacamole

Devilled eggs blend very well with guacamole. You can cook the dish for supper, dinner, side, or snack.

Servings: 6

Preparation time: 30 minutes

Ingredients:

- 6 whole eggs
- 1 tsp. mustard
- 1 tsp. hot sauce
- 1 tsp. Worcestershire sauce
- 2 ripe avocados
- 1 whole, red tomato, seeds out, cut into small dice
- 1 minced red onion
- 2 minced garlic cloves
- Juice of 1 lime
- 1 tsp. Salt
- 1 tsp. Black pepper

Directions:

In a boiling water pot, using a cooking spoon, carefully place the whole eggs. Do not drop them, or the shells might crack. Hard boil the eggs for 15 minutes.

When done, peel off the shells under cold running water and cut the eggs half lengthwise. Scoop out the hard yolks.

Slice the avocados into half, then eliminate the seed and scrape the avocado meat from its skin.

Place this in a food processor with the remaining ingredients. Add the yolks and mash them with a spoon. Season with salt and pepper.

Place back on top of each egg halves and serve.

13. Pomegranate Guacamole

Classic guacamole gets a fruity makeover with fresh cilantro and juicy arils. Prepare this for your loved ones and watch them marvel at your skills.

Servings: 6

Preparation time: 10 minutes

Ingredients:

- 2 halved, stoned & flesh scooped ripe avocados
- ½ tsp salt
- ½ tsp. black pepper
- ¼ c. chopped fresh cilantro
- ⅓ peeled & diced red onion
- ½ c. pomegranate arils
- 2 tbsps. fresh lime juice

Directions:

Mash the avocado in a bowl. Next, season the avocado well.

Add the cilantro, onion, pomegranate, lime juice, and salt and pepper. Stir until combined.

Serve straight away.

14. Prawn and Dill Guacamole

This guacamole blend with prawns is the perfect dip, snack, or appetizer for parties. Making this recipe is simple as the instructions are clear and easy to follow when preparing it.

Servings: 8

Preparation time: 9 minutes

Ingredients:

- 10½ oz. cooked, peeled & thinly sliced prawns
- 2 peeled, pitted & finely chopped ripe avocados
- 1 tbsp. freshly squeezed lime juice
- 2 tbsps. finely chopped dill
- 2 tsps. Salt
- 1 tsp. pepper

Directions:

Add the prawns, avocado, fresh lime juice, and dill to a bowl, gently tossing to combine.

Taste and season.

Transfer the mixture to a bowl, then serve.

15. Pumpkin Guacamole

Roasted pumpkin brings sweetness and color to this fiery pumpkin guacamole. It is suitable for your kids and adults as well.

Servings: 4

Preparation time: 10 minutes

Ingredients:

- 2 halved, stoned & mashed ripe avocados
- 1 tsp. olive oil
- ½ c. peeled & diced red onion
- 1 diced tomato
- ¼ c. chopped fresh cilantro
- 1 deseeded & diced jalapeno
- ¼ tsp. cumin
- 2 tbsps. freshly squeezed lime juice
- 2 c. diced roasted pumpkin
- ¼ tsp. Sea salt

Directions:

Combine the avocado, oil, onion, tomato, cilantro, jalapeno, cumin, and lime juice in a bowl.

Fold in the pumpkin and season to taste with salt.

Serve straight away.

16. Spring Pea and Mint Guacamole

This healthy avocado mash is sublime as a spread, delicious dip, and perfect as a pesto. It's your wake-up call to go green!

Servings: 1

Preparation time: 7 minutes

Ingredients:

- ¼ c. fresh spring peas
- ½ tsp coriander seeds
- 2 sprigs of mint leaves
- ¼ tsp. Sea salt
- ¼ tsp. Black pepper
- ⅓ peeled & pitted avocado
- 1 lemon wedge

Directions:

Blanch the pea pods for a few minutes in boiling water until cooked but al dente. Drain and set to one side.

In a pestle and mortar, grind the coriander seeds and the mint and a pinch of sea salt.

Add the peas to the pestle and mortar and gently mash.

In a second bowl, mash the avocado.

Add the pea-mint mixture to the avocado mash and with a fork, carefully combine.

Top with lemon juice and season with pepper to taste.

17. Summer Stone Fruit Guacamole

This gorgeous guacamole provides a real summer taste. Enjoy with spread-on wraps and tortilla chips, or enjoy with roasted or grilled chicken.

Servings: 6

Preparation time: 8 minutes

Ingredients:

- 2 ripe peeled & pitted avocados
- 3 tbsp freshly squeezed lime juice
- 1 tsp. Salt
- 1 c. pitted & diced sweet nectarines
- ½ c. pitted & diced ripe plums
- ½ c. peeled & diced red onion
- ¼ c. chopped fresh basil

Directions:

Add the avocados to a bowl, and with a fork, mash.

Add the fresh lime juice and a pinch of salt. Mix to combine.

Finally, add the nectarines, plums, onion, and basil, stirring to combine.

18. Toasted Pepita and Cotija Cheese Guacamole

Punchy cotija cheese ramps up the flavor as the toasted pumpkin seeds bring a crunch out to this guacamole dish. What you need for this recipe is lime juice, avocados, jalapeno pepper, red onion, cilantro, black pepper, salt, pepitas, and cotija cheese.

Servings: 6

Preparation time: 10 minutes

Ingredients:

- 2 tbsps. freshly squeezed lime juice
- 3 ripe peeled, stoned & mashed avocados
- ¼ c. seeded & diced jalapeno pepper
- ¼ c. peeled & diced red onion
- ½ c. chopped fresh cilantro
- ½ tsp. Salt
- ½ tsp. Black pepper
- 4 tbsps. crumbled cotija cheese
- ¼ c. toasted pepitas

Directions:

Combine the lime juice, avocado, jalapeno, red onion, and cilantro in a bowl.

Season with salt and black pepper.

Sprinkle over the cotija cheese and toasted pepitas, and serve straight away.

19. Tuna Guacamole

This guacamole with tuna is satisfying enough and tasty to eat all independently. However, you can as well serve it as an appetizer or snack.

Servings: 2

Preparation time: 10 minutes

Ingredients:

- ½ ripe peeled, stoned & mashed avocado
- 5 oz. can drained tuna in water
- Juice of ½ a medium lime
- ½ tsp. Cumin
- 1 tbsp. Chopped fresh cilantro
- 1 tbsp. Peeled & diced red onion
- ¼ c. Diced tomatoes
- ¼ tsp. Powdered garlic
- ¼ tsp. Salt
- ¼ tsp. Black pepper

Directions:

Combine the avocado, tuna, lime juice, cumin, cilantro, onion, tomatoes, and garlic in a bowl.

Season with salt and pepper, then serve it straight away.

20. Italian-Style Guacamole

For the love of Italian flavors, this guacamole comes out to be the top pick for guacamole recipes. It is easy to prepare as it takes only 10 minutes, and you can serve it on the table.

Servings: 4

Preparation time: 10 minutes

Ingredients:

- 3 ripe pitted & peeled avocados
- 2 tbsps. basil pesto
- ½ finely diced white onion
- 2 pressed garlic cloves
- 1 finely diced cherry tomato
- 1 tbsp. Fresh lemon juice
- ⅓ chopped fresh cilantro
- ¼ tsp. Ground cumin
- ½ tsp. Salt
- ¼ tsp. Black pepper
- 3 tbsp grated Parmesan cheese
- ½ c. Chopped fresh basil for garnish

Directions:

Mash avocados in a bowl.

Add pesto and mix well.

Add remaining ingredients except for half of cheese and basil and fold in well.

Garnish with remaining cheese and basil.

Serve guacamole.

21. Crab Guacamole

You can enrich a guacamole dish with crab meat as it will increase your preference for the dish. Serve it for breakfast or snack at any time of the day.

Servings: 4

Preparation time: 10 minutes

Ingredients:

- ¼ tsp. Black pepper
- ½ finely diced medium white onion
- ¼ tsp ground cumin
- ⅓ chopped fresh cilantro
- 3 pitted & peeled ripe avocados
- 2 pressed garlic cloves
- 1 tsp. Salt
- 6 oz can drained & flaked lump crabmeat
- 1 tbsp. fresh lime juice

Directions:

In a bowl, mash the avocados using a potato masher.

Add remaining ingredients and fold in well.

Serve guacamole.

22. Fajita Guacamole

Fajita and guacamole share cultural similarities. How about you merge both and see what you get? A fantastic and yummy mix!

Servings: 4

Preparation time: 15 minutes

Ingredients:

- ½ tsp olive oil
- ½ medium julienned red bell pepper
- ½ medium julienned green bell pepper
- ½ small julienned red onion
- 1 minced garlic clove
- ½ tsp. Salt
- ¼ tsp. Black pepper
- 3 pitted & peeled avocados
- 2 tsps. Fresh lime juice
- ¼ tsp. Onion powder
- ¼ tsp. Garlic powder
- ½ tsp. Cumin powder
- ½ tsp. paprika
- ⅓ crumbled queso fresco cheese

Directions:

In a skillet, heat the oil, then add the red and green bell peppers and onion. Sauté for 4 minutes until tender, and stir in garlic. Cook for 30 seconds until tender. Turn the heat off.

Mash avocados in a bowl.

Add remaining ingredients, including pepper mixture but leave a little cheese for garnish. Fold in well.

Garnish with cheese and serve guacamole.

23. Shrimp Guacamole

It is chunky guacamole that one can perfectly enjoy while in wraps. You can add hot sauce to add a kick to the meal.

Servings: 4

Preparation time: 10 minutes

Ingredients:

- 3 pitted, peeled, & diced ripe avocados
- ½ c. chopped cooked shrimp
- 1 finely diced red onion
- 1 deseeded & diced Roma tomato
- 1 cored & finely chopped jalapeno pepper
- 1 tbsp. lime juice, fresh
- ⅓ freshly chopped cilantro
- ¼ tsp. cumin, ground
- 1 tsp. hot sauce
- ½ tsp. Salt

Directions:

Using a bowl, add in avocados and the other ingredients, then mix well.

Set in serving plates and enjoy.

24. Black Bean Guacamole

You may not have heard of beans in guacamole, but try it out with black beans, and you'll be impressed. The aroma and taste are exceptional.

Servings: 4

Preparation time: 10 minutes

Ingredients:

- 3 ripe pitted & peeled avocados
- ½ finely diced medium red onion
- ⅓ chopped fresh cilantro
- 15 oz. can drained & rinsed black beans
- 2 pressed garlic cloves
- ¼ tsp. ground cumin
- 1 tbsp. fresh lime juice
- 1 tsp. Salt
- ½ tsp. Black pepper

Directions:

Mash avocados in a bowl.

Add the remaining ingredients and mix well.

Serve guacamole.

25. Strawberry Guacamole

This guacamole is so feminine. It is an enticing way to enjoy guacamole dishes throughout the year.

Servings: 4

Preparation time: 10 minutes

Ingredients:

- 3 pitted & peeled ripe avocados
- 1 cored & finely chopped jalapeno pepper
- 1 tbsp. lime juice, fresh
- 1 tbsp. Orange juice
- ⅓ freshly chopped cilantro
- ¼ tsp. cumin, ground
- ½ tsp. Salt
- ½ c. chopped strawberries

Directions:

Using a bowl and a potato masher, add in avocados and mash well.

Add the rest of the ingredients leaving only half the strawberries and mix well.

Top the mixture with remaining strawberries and serve.

26. Guacamole Hummus

What better way to enhance hummus than infuse it with avocado? Now, you are drooling over that already. Try it out today!

Servings: 4

Preparation time: 10 minutes

Ingredients:

- 2 pitted & peeled small avocados
- 1 sliced jalapeno pepper
- 2 tbsps. tahini
- 2 pressed garlic cloves
- 1 (15 oz.) can drained & rinsed chickpeas
- 2 tbsps. Fresh cilantro leaves + extra for garnish
- ¼ c. fresh lime juice
- ¼ tsp. Salt
- 2 tbsps. Extra virgin olive oil for serving

Directions:

Add the ingredients to a food processor, then process until they become smooth.

Pour guacamole into a bowl, then drizzle with olive oil.

Next, garnish with cilantro leaves.

27. Chicken & Guacamole Tostadas

It is rare to a person who does not love chicken. Merging it with guacamole adds more taste and flavor. Enjoy the recipe!

Servings: 4

Preparation time: 8 minutes

Ingredients:

- 1 serving Super Simple Guacamole
- 2 c. shredded skinless, boneless rotisserie chicken breast
- 1/4 tsp. smoked paprika
- 8 (6") corn tostada shells
- ½ finely chopped romaine lettuce
- 1 tbsp. freshly squeezed lime juice
- ½ salsa of choice

Directions:

Toss together chicken, lime juice, and paprika in a bowl. Spread guacamole over tostada shell. Sprinkle chopped lettuce on the tostada. Top each tostada with 1/4 c. chicken and about 2 tbsps. salsa. Enjoy!

28. Honey & Raisin Guacamole Dessert

This dessert pairs wonderfully with Ezekiel bread, freshly sliced vegetables, or blue corn tortilla chips. Remember to choose a ripe avocado for incredible results.

Servings: 4

Preparation time: 10 minutes

Ingredients:

- 4 avocados
- ¼ chopped yellow onion
- 1 minced garlic clove
- 1 tbsp. vanilla
- ¼ c. organic raisins
- 2 tbsps. raw honey

Directions:

In a blender, pulse together raisins and honey. Scrape sides of the blender to remove mixture; set aside. Mash avocados. Mix honey and raisin mixture with avocados. Combine with onion and garlic. Stir in vanilla.

Serve after mixing the ingredients well.

29. Sweet Guacamole Dessert

When you have 7 minutes to prepare a good dessert dish, this recipe should be on your mind. You can have it with the fruit juice of your choice.

Servings: 2

Preparation time: 7 minutes

Ingredients:

- 2 small avocados
- 4 tbsps. whipping cream
- 3 tbsps. powdered sugar
- ¼ freshly squeezed lemon
- 2 tsps. cinnamon
- ½ c. chopped strawberries
- ½ c. crushed vanilla wafers

Directions:

Blend avocados in a blender. Add whipping cream, powdered sugar, lemon, and cinnamon and blend until creamy. Chill mixture for one hour. Place into a serving bowl and crumble crushed vanilla wafers on top. Serve with a side of chopped strawberries.

30. Guacamole Veggie Wraps

If you are a vegan or love greens, this is the perfect guacamole recipe. It is super easy with good follow-through instructions.

Servings: 4

Preparation time: 10 minutes

Ingredients:

- 1 serving Super Simple Guacamole
- 2 tbsps. chopped cilantro
- ¼ small jalapeño pepper, seeds removed
- 1/8 tsp. chili powder
- 3 chopped Roma tomatoes
- 5 oz. chopped cabbage
- 2 medium scallions
- 1 small red pepper, cored & cut into small slabs
- 1 peeled carrot
- ¼ tsp. salt
- 4 tortillas

Directions:

In a food processor, lightly chop cilantro, jalapeno, cabbage, scallions, red pepper, carrot, chili powder, and salt; set aside. On a serving plate, place the tortilla flat. Spread guacamole evenly on the tortilla. Add in vegetable mixture. Sprinkle tomato on top. Wrap tightly and serve.

31. Lemon Pepper Shrimp and Guacamole Rolls

Shrimp and guacamole go well together, especially as party snacks. What is keeping you from tasting greatness?

Servings: 4

Preparation time: 10 minutes

Ingredients:

- 1 serving Fresh Basil Guacamole
- 8 mini bread rolls, about 2½" in diameter, sliced in half
- 2 freshly squeezed lemons
- ½ tsp. white pepper
- 16 jumbo size cooked & deveined shrimp
- ¼ tsp. Paprika

Directions:

Remove and discard some middle layer of each roll to create a bowl shape.

In a bowl, stir lemon juice and white pepper. Place a small dollop of guacamole on each bread bowl.

One at a time, dip a jumbo shrimp into the lemon/pepper mixture and place it on top of the guacamole.

Lightly sprinkle paprika over each shrimp to season.

32. Guacamole Deviled Eggs

When you add eggs to any recipe, it becomes tastier. So, try this recipe for breakfast to kickstart your day well.

Servings: 3

Preparation time: 5 minutes

Ingredients:

- 1 serving Bacon & Tomato Guacamole
- 6 large hard-boiled eggs
- 1 tsp. Chili pepper

Directions:

Allow hard-boiled eggs to cool, and cut each egg in half horizontally. Scoop out yolks and set them aside. With a small spoon, dollop guacamole into each halved egg. Sprinkle with chili powder on top to taste.

33. Mushroom & Guacamole Tacos

Mixing avocado and mushroom makes the best guacamole recipe. The guacamole is good if you take it as a snack, side dish, or even a healthy breakfast.

Servings: 2

Preparation time: 25 minutes

Ingredients:

- 1 serving Tex-Mex Ranger Guacamole
- 2 tsps. vegetable oil
- 1 chopped garlic clove
- ¼ c. white onion
- 4 oz. cremini mushrooms
- 4 oz. oyster mushrooms
- 4 corn tortillas,
- ½ c. warmed queso fresco
- 1 tsp. Salt

Directions:

Heat 1 tsp. of oil in a large. Sauté onion until soft, about 5 minutes.

Add garlic and continue to sauté until garlic is golden brown. Transfer to a bowl and set aside.

Heat remaining oil in a pan. Add half of the mushrooms, then cook until golden brown. Once cooked, remove and set aside.

Add remaining mushrooms and cook until golden brown. Combine all mushrooms and season with salt. Mix with onion and garlic mixture.

Place each tortilla flat on a plat and spread guacamole. Add mushroom mixture. Lastly, add on top warm crumbled queso fresco.

34. Kyle's Smokey Chardonnay Guacamole

Cooking should not be basic; instead, you should try new recipes once in a while. This Kyle's Smokey Chardonnay guacamole is worth your cooking time. Not only is it sweet but also a perfect snack for parties.

Servings: 2

Preparation time: 5 minutes

Ingredients:

- 2 avocados
- ½ chopped yellow onion,
- 1 minced garlic clove
- 2 diced Roma tomatoes
- 1 freshly squeezed lemon
- 2 tbsps. Oaky white wine chardonnay
- ½ tsp. Kosher salt
- ½ tsp. Pepper

Directions:

Mash avocados. Add onion, garlic, and tomatoes. Stir in lemon juice and wine. Season it with pepper and salt.

35. Ensalada De Guacamole

The guacamole recipe should be on your menu; if not twice a week, then once will do. The dish is healthy and delicious too.

Servings: 3

Preparation time: 15 minutes

Ingredients:

- 6 bacon slices
- 3 tbsps. vegetable oil
- 1 tbsp. vinegar
- ½ tsp. salt
- 1/8 tsp. pepper
- 3 drops of red pepper sauce
- 2 peeled & cubed avocados
- 2 chopped tomatoes,
- 1 chopped onion
- Salad greens

Directions:

Bring the oil to heat in a pan, then fry the bacon. Drain the bacon on a paper towel and break it into pieces.

Blend the oil, vinegar, salt, pepper, and red pepper sauce.

Toss the mixture with the avocados, and stir in the bacon, tomatoes, and onion.

Chill for 2 hours. Serve over the salad greens.

36. Garbonzo Guacamole Dip

The beans and guacamole blend are superb and sweet. This recipe will leave your family wanting more as it is an addictive dip that goes well with most meals.

Servings: 6

Preparation time: 4 minutes

Ingredients:

- 1 (8 oz.) drained garbanzo beans
- 2 tbsps. lemon juice
- 1 minced garlic clove
- ½ c. red onion
- 1 ripe peeled & cubed avocado
- ½ c. dairy sour cream
- 1 (4 oz.) can green mild chilies, diced & undrained Dash of hot pepper sauce and cumin
- 1 chopped tomato

Directions:

Mix the beans, lemon juice, and garlic in a blender for 10 seconds. Then, add everything but the tomatoes. Blend until smooth for another 45 seconds.

Chill before serving. Garnish with the tomatoes.

37. Green Chili Pepper Guacamole

Hot guacamole might be one of your next favorite recipes. You can tweak it to your liking to accommodate more servings.

Servings: 4

Preparation time: 5 minutes

Ingredients:

- 4 mashed avocados
- ½ c. finely chopped green chili peppers
- ¼ c. minced onion
- 1 tsp. salt
- ¼ c. lemon juice

Directions:

Blend all ingredients. Chill covered before serving.

38. Guacamole Cocktail Spread

Want to have a taste of a delicious guacamole spread? This cocktail spread comes out unique and is easy to prepare.

Servings: 4

Preparation time: 10 minutes

Ingredients:

- 1 lb. avocado
- 1 tbsp. grated onion
- 1 tbsp. chili sauce
- 1 grated garlic clove
- ½ tsp. Salt

Directions:

Slice the avocados in half, then scoop out the fruit so that the skin stays intact.

Mix all ingredients with the avocado. Season to taste.

Scoop mixture into avocado skins.

Chill and serve.

39. Guacamole Colombo

If you want to try experimenting with your guacamole recipe, this is the to-go- recipe. It is simple to prepare and takes only 5 minutes.

Servings: 1

Preparation time: 5 minutes

Ingredients:

- 1 lb. ripe avocado
- 1 c. chopped tomato
- ¼ c. chopped green pepper
- 1 tsp. chili powder
- 1 tsp. onion salt
- 1 tbsp. lime juice
- 1 tbsp. olive oil
- 1 c. plain yogurt

Directions:

Add yogurt to the mashed avocados, so they keep longer. Mix all ingredients, and serve.

40. Guacamole Cream Soup

This soup is thick and good for your kids. You can prepare it as an appetizer or a side dish.

Servings: 3

Preparation time: 8 minutes

Ingredients:

- 1 lb. peeled & pitted avocado
- 1 sliced onion
- 1 c. heavy cream
- 1 tsp. Instant chicken base
- ½ tsp. salt
- 3 drops red pepper seasoning
- 2 c. milk

Directions:

Mix the avocado with onion and ½ c. cream in a blender. Add remaining cream, instant chicken base, seasoning, and milk to stir in. Chill before serving.

41. Broccoli Guacamole

Broccoli is sweet and guacamole too is lovely. So, combining the two makes the vegetable mixture very delicious and is a healthy diet.

Servings: 2

Preparation time: 5 minutes

Ingredients:

- 1 c. chopped, cooked & cooled broccoli
- 1 avocado
- ¼ c. sour cream
- ¼ c. mayonnaise
- 2 tbsps. Parmesan cheese, grated
- ¼ c. Cheddar cheese, grated
- 1 tsp. Green onion, minced
- ½ tsp. Curry powder
- ¼ tsp. salt
- 1 squeeze of lemon juice

Directions:

Use a blender to puree all ingredients. Chill before serving.

42. Best-ever Guacamole

Are you confused about what snack or appetizer to prepare? Try this simple guacamole recipe as it only takes 6 minutes to prepare, and you will love the outcome.

Servings: 3

Preparation time: 6 minutes

Ingredients:

- 4 ripe mashed avocados
- 1 chopped tomato
- 1 chopped onion
- 1 tsp. Salt
- ½ tsp. Celery salt
- ¼ tsp. Pepper
- ¼ tsp. ground cumin
- ½ c. Lemon juice
- 1 c. Prepared horseradish Picante sauce

Directions:

Blend the avocados, tomato, and onion. Use salt, celery salt, pepper, cumin, lemon juice, horseradish, and Picante to season to taste.

43. Best Guacamole Dip

This dip is creamy and tasty. You need to try it out as you only need avocados, tomato, onion, lemon juice, salt, sour cream, pepper, and salt.

Servings: 6

Preparation time: 7 minutes

Ingredients:

- 5 very ripe avocados
- 1 chopped tomato
- ½ c. finely chopped onion
- 2 tsps. lemon juice
- 1 tsp. garlic salt
- 1 c. sour cream
- 2 tsps. Salt
- 1 tsp. Pepper

Directions:

Mash the avocados with lemon juice. Stir in sour cream and seasonings. Stir until creamy. Mix in onion and tomato to serve.

44. Blender Guacamole

This recipe is among the simplest to make. All you need is a blender, and you are good to go.

Servings: 5

Preparation time: 5 minutes

Ingredients:

- 2 ripe sliced avocados
- 2 tbsp. onion
- 1¼ tbsps. Lemon juice
- ½ tsp. chili powder
- 1/3 c. mayonnaise
- 1 small tomato

Directions:

In a blender, pour all the ingredients, then process until they become smooth.

45. California Guacamole

Nothing is as delicious as guacamole that you make from California avocados. They turn out well and are very delicious.

Servings: 4

Preparation time: 8 minutes

Ingredients:

- 1½ tbsps. fresh lemon juice
- 2 minced garlic cloves
- 2 ripe peeled & diced California avocados
- 1 tsp. dried and crushed leaf basil
- ¼ c. finely diced red pepper
- 2 tbsps. Salsa
- 1½ tbsps. slivered almonds, chopped coarsely
- 2 tbsps. green onion, thinly sliced
- ¼ c. Dollop sour cream garnish
- ½ tsp. salt
- 1 tbsp. cilantro, minced

Directions:

Blend 1 avocado and lemon juice. Add in basil, garlic, salt and cilantro.

Use remaining avocado to dice and stir into the mixture. Next, stir in almonds, red pepper, green onion and salsa.

Use sour cream to garnish. Serve.

46. Guacamole Bean Casserole Dip

Preparing a guacamole dip is simple, and even a beginner in the kitchen can make it. First, you need to combine all your ingredients, and you are good to go.

Servings: 4

Preparation time: 6 minutes

Ingredients:

- 1 can (16 oz.) of refried beans
- ½ can (4 oz.) of green chiles, chopped
- 1½ c. guacamole, chilled
- 1 jar (16 oz.) Ortega green chili salsa
- ¼ tsp. Grated Cheddar cheese

Directions:

Heat the beans and green chiles in a small pan. Add layers of beans, guacamole, salsa, and chiles to a casserole dish. Sprinkle with cheese to serve.

47. Guacamole Burgers

Burgers with guacamole filling turn out very delicious. You can take the burgers for breakfast, dinner, or a snack.

Servings: 3

Preparation time: 15 minutes

Ingredients:

- 1 lb. ground beef
- ½ c. Old El Paso taco shells, crushed
- 1/3 c. milk
- ½ tsp. onion salt
- 15 peeled, seeded & chopped tomatoes
- 1 c. guacamole
- 5 hamburger buns, split, toasted & buttered

Directions:

Combine the beef, crushed taco shells, milk, and onion salt. Make the mixture into patties, and grill for 5 minutes on each side.

Add tomato while stirring. Spread guacamole over each burger, and serve on buns.

48. Nicole's Amazing Guacamole

Making guacamole in Nicole's style makes it come out delicious and more straightforward. In the preparation, just combine all your ingredients.

Servings: 4

Preparation time: 6 minutes

Ingredients:

- 4 avocados
- 2 tbsps. olive oil
- ½ small onion, minced
- 2 small cloves garlic, minced
- 1 small Finely chopped tomato
- 1 tbsp. Finely chop cilantro
- ½ tsp. cumin
- ½ c. sour cream
- 1 tbsp. Lime juice

Directions:

Mix all ingredients well and serve.

49. Vegetable Guacamole

Do you want to go all green in the preparation of guacamole? This healthy meal is delicious.

Servings: 2

Preparation time: 6 minutes

Ingredients:

- 1 avocado, mashed
- 4 pieces chopped lettuce
- 1 chopped celery stick peeled
- 1 cube frozen garlic melted
- 1 frozen artichoke heart

Directions:

Combine the lettuce and avocado well. Mix in all the remaining ingredients and serve.

50. Ambrosia South American Guacamole

Do you want to have a feel of South American cuisine? Then, this Ambrosia Guacamole will fulfill your needs. Try it any day and time for a perfect snack.

Servings: 2

Preparation time: 6 minutes

Ingredients:

- 2 ripe peeled & seeded avocados
- ¼ tsp. ground cumin
- ½ medium Roma tomato, seeded, diced
- ¼ c. sweet white onion, minced
- 1 aji chili
- ¼ cilantro, chopped
- 2 tbsps. Fresh lime juice
- ¼ tsp. Hot pepper sauce
- ¼ tsp. Sea salt
- ¼ tsp. Pepper

Directions:

Cut avocado in large chunks, then mash it coarsely in a bowl with a fork.

Add remaining ingredients, then blend gently.

Taste it, then adjust the seasoning with more pepper sauce, pepper, and salt.

51. Tomato - Salsa Guacamole

This recipe needs avocados, lime juice, salsa, tomato, cilantro, salt, and pepper. It is a healthy blend and turns out superb.

Servings: 3

Preparation time: 5 minutes

Ingredients:

- 2 small avocados
- 1½ tsps. lime juice
- 1 tbsp. salsa
- 2 tbsps. tomatoes, diced
- 1 tbsp. Cilantro, shredded
- ½ tsp. Salt
- ¼ tsp. Pepper

Directions:

Peel and mash the avocados.

Mix in all ingredients.

52. Cajun Guacamole

It is a three-step instruction recipe that takes only 7 minutes to prepare. It is delicious and an excellent snack for kids.

Servings: 8

Preparation time: 7 minutes

Ingredients:

- ½ tsp. Cayenne pepper
- 4 avocados
- 1 thinly sliced scallion bunch
- 5 finely chopped large garlic cloves
- 2 tsps. Chopped fresh thyme
- ¼ c. fresh lemon juice
- 1 tsp. salt
- 1 finely chopped green bell pepper
- 1½ c. halved & quartered cherry tomatoes,
- 1 tsp. Hot paprika
- ½ tsp. Celery salt
- ½ c. Tortilla chips for serving

Directions:

In a bowl, mash the salt, juice, and avocados.

Add the remaining ingredients and mix well.

Serve the guacamole with the tortilla chips.

53. Choice Mango Chipotle Guacamole

Any guacamole with mango does not go wrong, especially when using the tasty Mexican avocado. In addition, it is also a healthy dish.

Servings: 4

Preparation time: 6 minutes

Ingredients:

- 2 ripe Mexican avocados, peeled and pitted
- 1 peeled, pitted & diced mango
- 1 small minced garlic clove
- 1 tbsp. chopped fresh cilantro leaves
- 2 tsps. Lime juice
- ¼ tsp. Ground dried chipotle pepper
- ½ tsp. Salt

Directions:

Mash avocados in a bowl.

Add the chipotle powder, garlic, lime juice, mango, cilantro, and salt into the bowl.

Serve immediately.

54. Heavenly Guasacaca - Guacamole from Venezuela

Want to try a Venezuela dish? This recipe will give you a taste of a Venezuelan guacamole taste and feel.

Servings: 4

Preparation time: 7 minutes

Ingredients:

- 2 avocados
- 1 green pepper
- 3 garlic cloves
- ½ c. chopped onion
- 1 tbsp. vegetable oil
- 3 tbsps. Vinegar
- ¼ c. chopped parsley
- ½ tsp. Salt
- ¼ tsp. Pepper
- 1 medium chili pepper
- ¼ c. Chopped tomato

Directions:

Chop the avocados and the green pepper, then place them in a bowl with the onion.

Finely chop the garlic and chili pepper, then pour the mixture into the bowl.

Add the vinegar, vegetable oil, tomato, and parsley and toss gently.

55. Inviting Fruity Guacamole

If you like avocados, you will fall in love with this fruity guacamole. The blend with pomegranate seeds makes it a delicious fix for any occasion.

Servings: 8

Preparation time: 6 minutes

Ingredients:

- 1 peeled, pitted & diced avocado
- 1 ½ tsps. minced red onion
- 1 tsp. minced seeded serrano chili
- 12 red grapes, halved
- ½ c. fresh diced peaches
- 2 tsps. Salt
- 2 tbsps. Pomegranate seeds

Directions:

Gently mash the avocado with the onion and serrano pepper in a bowl.

Mix in the grapes and peaches.

Season with salt and, if desired, garnish with pomegranate seeds to serve.

56. Tantalizing Haphazard Guacamole

It is a tasty guacamole recipe that takes only 8 minutes to prepare. Try it any time, be it for breakfast, dessert or dinner.

Servings: 4

Preparation time: 8 minutes

Ingredients:

- 1 avocado
- 4 tbsps. mild salsa
- 3 tbsps. lime juice
- 2 tbsps. chopped cilantro
- 1 largish garlic clove, minced
- ¼ tsp. cumin
- 3 tbsps. finely chopped tomatoes

Directions:

Mash avocado well, and add everything else to taste!

Conclusion

Those were some of the best guacamole recipes that you can use as a reference when you are preparing this dish in your home. Try them out. By making authentic and delicious guacamole, you will be able to impress your friends or guests with a recipe that they haven't tried before. This is a dish that can be prepared in a number of varieties, but all of them will provide an amazingly tasty meal to your taste buds.

About the Author

Owen isn't your typical cookbook writer. He built a life and career as a successful stockbroker in New York for many years, getting into the routine of it all. He enjoyed the crazy schedule, his exploding inbox, and endless phone conversations with clients. Still, he always found himself in the kitchen when he had some time to spare. Even if he got home at 11:00 pm and had an early morning meeting the next day, he always cooked delicious meals and dinners for himself.

When the pandemic hit and lots of his clients started pulling out, Owen began to question whether he would even have a job within the next couple of months. Once the world went into lockdown, his job became harder with the sudden obstacles of working from home with a job like his. His stress, however, was very fruitful because it often resulted in new dishes.

More than a home office, at one point, his place felt more like a restaurant. Whether it was breakfast, lunch, or dinner, he was always whipping up something amazing! When he was let go, he was relieved to finally have more time to work on new recipes to share with his friends and family. Eventually, they encouraged him to start writing cookbooks… and that's how he began his new life as an amateur cook and cookbook writer. Now, he travels across the US searching for inspiration for his recipes, but he always finds his way back home to his cozy townhouse in New Jersey, ready to share all of his new dishes with his loved ones.

Appendices

Thank you ♥

Hey, guys! I just wanted to say thanks for supporting me by purchasing one of my e-books. I have to say—when I first started writing cookbooks, I didn't have many expectations for myself because it was never a part of "the plan." It was more of a hobby, something I did for me and decided to put out there if someone might click on my book and buy it because they liked my food. Well, let me just say it's been a while since those days, and it's been a wild journey!

Now, cookbook writing is a huge part of my life, and I'm doing things I love! So, THANK YOU for trusting me with your weekly meal preps, weekend BBQs, 10-minute dinners, and all of your special occasions. If it weren't for you, I wouldn't be able to concentrate on producing all sorts of delicious recipes, which is why I've decided to reach out and ask for your help. What kind of recipes would you like to see more of? Are you interested in special diets, foods made with kitchen appliances, or just easy recipes on a time-crunch? Your input will help me create books you want to read with recipes you'll actually make! Make sure to let me know, and your suggestions could trigger an idea for my next book…

Take care!

Owen

Printed in Great Britain
by Amazon

3086d445-31ad-4b02-bea6-9fce3841ecb2R01